To My Favorite Sister With Love: Melissa's Memory Book

To My Favorite Sister With Love: Melissa's Memory Book

By Stephanie Fava

Copyright © 2012 by Stephanie Fava.

Library of Congress Control Number: 2012912221
ISBN: Hardcover 978-1-4771-4057-4
Softcover 978-1-4771-4056-7
Ebook 978-1-4771-4058-1

All rights reserved. No part of this book may be reproduced or transmitted in any form or by any means, electronic or mechanical, including photocopying, recording, or by any information storage and retrieval system, without permission in writing from the copyright owner.

This book was printed in the United States of America.

To order additional copies of this book, contact:
Xlibris Corporation
1-888-795-4274
www.Xlibris.com
Orders@Xlibris.com
118950

Contents

Introduction to my sister Melissa Fava

My favorite sister with love 21
About my sister Melissa 23
In the Beginning 25
Things to remember about Melissa 27
Recollections 29
My sister my mom and I in the kitchen 31
My sister's wisdom 33

My sister's gift 35
About myself 37
School days 39
After School 41
Melissa's Room 43
Boys 45
Sometimes it's the little things 47
Me, myself, and all the angels and gadgets in between 49
The love song of j. Agnes prufrock* 53

- Melissa Fava
- Birthday: October 30 1987

Date she Died November 24, 2007

With Love from your Sister Stephanie marie Fava

To my sister Melissa ashley fava

To my favortite sister, with Love

Written by Stephanie Fava

Melissas memory book

To My sister melissa, who encouraged me to dream, I wanted to thank you my dreams came true.

My favorite sister with love

This is a journal about you and me, sister to sister. Its my gift to you. It may be the most precious gift I will ever be able to give you. I've filled it with love and the important recollections of a lifetime to help you understand who I am why you,ve become the special person you are.

Its my hope you will want to read this book from time to time whenever you,d like to reminisece. Each event I've written about, every feeling, is a place in the intricate mosaic which is our relationship. I don't know why some memories shine like bright pennies and others dim and disappear, but they do. Its the bright shining pennies of our life together that I've written about.

With love

About my sister Melissa

My sister apron pockets were crammed with important objects.... an assortment of barrettes, marbles and puzzle pieces awaiting return to their proper places. Shoe laces which I had tied in triple knots and strung from the handle on my dresser's top drawer to the knob on my closet and back again.

Why are tiny fragments like these among my favorite recollections of my sister? Why is it so important to include her in a book dedicated to my sister? Because she is part of me and I'm a part of her. My story cannot be complete without Melissa.

In the Beginning

As a child I marveled at how my sister Melissa knew just how to mend my scraped knees, she was always there with a handkerchief and, had the uncanny ability to read my mind. She put on that knowing smile and I knew I was safe in her keeping.

As long as she was nearby all would be right in the world. A good night kiss, her encouraging smile, her wisdom, the softness of her embrace, the scent of her as she'd come into a room. These are trucked lovingly among my childhood souvenirs. Melissa always knew how many peas were left on my plate, and whether or not i had used toothpaste. She seemed to know when i was really sick or i was just hoping to avoid another math test. And when i felt like the whole world was against me she was there to say "I know you can do it".

Things to remember about Melissa

I will always remember my sister laughter every time she showered. She would take music in the bathroom with her and belt out the turns. She thought she had a great voice, but it drove me crazy.

I will always remember Melissa's contagious smile. She would light up any room that she walked into. Melissa also named her stuffed animal monkey Amico after our dog.

Recollections

When I think about growing up with my sister Melissa, It's all the little things about her that pop into my mind. Most seem unimportant by themselves but there are so many, I realize how closely I must have been observing her. I knew instinctively how she would react to almost anything I said whether she would smile or frown or say nothing. These are some of my best memories of those days.

My sister my mom and I in the kitchen

There we, side by side, tasted creating, giggling and having fun. Those were the days! "What do you think it needs"? Melissa would ask "more chocolate," I invariably replied, even if we were making a roast. Or she would plead, "I can't figure out how much is three quarters of a cup." That's how i learned fractions.

My mother's kitchen was a place for solving problems whenever I had something especially difficult to discuss I would wait until we were baking bread. Then, she would listen, not saying much, but I could tell how she felt by watching the way she kneaded-should I say pouded the dough.

My sister's wisdom

My sisters Melissa consider herself wise, but whether she knew it or not, she was a teacher. Her greatest course was courage. The lessons were always delivered quietly and without embellishment, "follow your heart, nothing impossible." Or, she would encourage, "don't hold back, the real tragedy isn't failure, but wondering what might have been."

My sister's gift

Maybe it's the way you tilt your head when perplexed, or that slow sweet smile of yours. Perhaps it's the determination you show whenever faced with a difficult situation. Whatever it is, sometimes you remind me so much of mom.

About myself

I remember reaching an age when images of my future began to take shape in my mind it happened almost every night. I had been content wearing jeans, climbing trees and never giving a thought to the next day. Suddenly, I wanted only pretty clothes and clear cut blueprint into the future. One day I would imagine becoming a ballerina, the next day I wanted to raise horses. Sometimes I visualize myself traveling the world, other times spending my days in a small cottage with a thatched roof and a cozy fireplace, would I be an actress or a teacher.? Would I fall in love?

School days

Here's a story Melissa told me once. When she first went to school she planted a tree on Arbor Day just like the kids did almost everywhere, she recently to that school and learned they had cut down her tree.... It had grown too big. Guess how that made my sister feel.

After School

Every day after school Melissa would be met by her faithful friend Sean, the white cocker spaniel who never seemed to mind when Melissa dressed in her sun bonnets and frilly dresses and crawled into her basket. When she went to kindergarten Sean would see Melissa and walk her to the door in the morning and greet Melissa at the door on my return.

Melissa's Room

Melissa room was her safe haven. There she could play her music, hang her pictures, collect her stuff and rearrange her closet into umpteen new outfits. There she could stare out of her window into her future while looking out over the houses nearby and feeling safe and secure. I don't think she has ever felt so protected.

Boys

Did you ever stop to consider how when you're five years old you get along just fine with boys? But soon they start pulling your hair and playing war so you play with dolls. Then they start to like you again but not your dolls. Its a difficult choice.

Sometimes it's the little things

Learning to drive a car one of, the highlight of my sister Melissa's life but it's true. She was more excited about graduating from school rather then, getting her driver's license, its it amazing how much space in our heart we allow the simple joys and sometimes the anguish of growing up.

Me, myself, and all the angels and gadgets in between

Lord, thank you for the gift of life and of family and friends. Thank you for giving me a roof over my head, and of course thanks for giving me me. Amen. I was once asked what is important to me and i had so many things to answer with i just said me, myself, and all the angels and gadgets in between. In my life, my experiences had led me to believe that the big things are sometimes just as important as the little things, if not more important. The little things of course being a good home, food and water, and clean air as well as all those other necessities of life. I call these gadgets because they are the tools of life that make life so much more bearable. The big things, my angels, keep me going, lend a hand, and show me love. My family of course, who when time calls for desperate measures, always seem to find time for one another.

My friends, who laugh, cry and get mad with because no one else in in the most important thing in the world to me, is Melissa. She's the one that keeps me going because she understands me more than anyone else in the world and has been with me since i was born. She is my best friend that cries, and laughs with me because she feels everything I feel. Who do you ask is this girl, she is myself. The greatest gift anyone can give themselves is themselves and the most important thing is to love oneself, more than anyone else. The most important things to me are me, myself, and the angels and gadgets in between.

Written By
Melissa Fava

The love song of j. Agnes prufrock*

The planes fly by as I wait for you under the night sky with all my being I hope today is the day, the day you will come and stay. I see you, but you don't see me. Is it my hair, my looks, my face? Do i dare ask, for you to stay? Stay for you, stay for me, stay for love that can somehow be. It is fast approaching the time, for me to say my good-byes. My heart is with you, it will never leave, like a mother is never separated from her family. You stand up and move with the line. I remain seated, never inching nearer. You cannot leave without knowing me love, knowing how all those nights i cried for you, waited for you. What would i do if you laughed at my sight? Because i am not witty, charming, or beautiful. I am me. O how i wish you liked me for me.

Why did you leave? Now the times i held your hand, as we lay kissing beneath the sand, in my dream, but they will never come true. What is that a tear? I have cried rivers, which will now turn into oceans. Farewell my love. I hope today would be the day, the day you would come and stay.

Written By
Melissa Fava